MONTGOMERY HALL

by

DORIS H. MASI

Published by
Canal Side Publishers
R.F.D. 3 - Box 137
Frankfort, NY   13340

Printed in U.S.A.
by Steffen Press
Holland Patent, NY

Library of Congress
Catalog Number
94-69573
ISBN 0-9628208-9-X

Other Works
by
Doris H. Masi

Keesler's Corners
Pride O'The Hilltop
Merrick's View

PREFACE

Montgomery Hall, constructed during the early years of the 19th century, has shared fully in the community life of Fort Plain, N.Y.

In the early days of the Erie Canal, it was known as "Bowen's Tavern", later called Montgomery Hall. The Farmers & Mechanics Bank, locating in the building after its hotel days, had the clock tower and other modifications added in 1892.

Montgomery Hall also accommodated at various times a United States Post Office, various club headquarters and professional offices. At the present time, it is home to a gift and book shop, florist shop and law offices, as well as offering apartments on the second and third floors.

Over 150 years of social and business life of Fort Plain are intimately associated with this venerable building.

"Bonnie Eloise", the song that George Elliott wrote for his fiancee, Mary Eloise Bowen, was used by both sides of the conflict in the Civil War.

DHM

CAST OF CHARACTERS

Millicent Cooper (Two-Bits) -
        bound girl
Molly Maguire-
        #1 maid at the Hall
Daisy Bogardus-
        cook and Isaiah, her husband
Mrs. Phidia Smith-
        star boarder
Johnny Dawley-
        apprentice attorney
George Elliott-
        embryonic newsman
Audolph Hearst-
        crack reporter for
        The Daily Sun (NYC)
Solomon and Eve Bowen-
        proprieters of the Hall
Mary Eloise and Anna-
        their daughters
The Count of Malamocco-
        Ambassador
Julius Higgins-
        stablemaster
Livingston Van Alstyne-
        bar tender par excellence
Abijah Smith-
        hill farmer
Sarah Hearst, Dolph's mother,
    Rosina Myers, her personal maid,
    Mr. & Mrs. Biermann, entrepre-
    neurs, Joe Simms, attorney,
    Washington Rayburn and Napoleon
    Jones, Hall employees, Lizzie
    Higgins, laundress and Elvira
    Dawley, Johnny's mother. Also
    Vincenzo and Antonio, drivers for
    the Count and four footmen, and
    Ame, outlaw and Neva Root.
In absentia: LEVI HIRSCH, itinerate
    traveling merchant. Lorenzo Root,
    hill farmer
Time: May, 1857

MONTGOMERY HALL
by Doris Masi

CHAPTER 1

"Strange goin's on," Millie Cooper told herself silently. "Gettin' me up way early, havin' me lug that big kettle of hot 'taters out to the barn and nearly breakin' my neck stumblin' over ever' blessed rock there was, in the dark."

"On top o' that, packin' me off without so much as by your leave!"

Aloud, the 14 year-old spoke up to the dark form of the driver seated beside her on the light spring wagon. "No breakfast, neither, Abijah!"

"Hush up, girl," the man responded; "Ye'll git some vittles when we git to town."

Millie sank further down on the wagon seat, pulling her shawl closely around her thin shoulders. There was a chill in the early May morning and though the false dawn was appearing, the birds had not yet begun their customary serenade.

Millie felt terribly alone. Unable to keep still, she finally commented "I kin see we ain't headed for the Mills. Are we shun-pikin', Ab?"

Hesitating briefly, Abijah replied "Ye ain't so dumb as folks make out, air ye?" He laughed shortly and went on "Ye're right, We ain't takin' the corduroy. Anyhow, I ain't supposed to visit with you no more'n what's needful, so jest cogitate on how ye can git along with the folks ye'll be workin' for.

"How can I do that when I don't even know who they are?" shot back Millie, indignantly.

"Well," again Abijah hesitated; "I guess there's no harm in apprizin' ye o' that much. They're hotel folks in Fort Plain and they been lookin' for a replacement for one o' their help. Miz Root figured you'd fill the bill bein' she don't need you no more. Now, no more gabbin'," and he flicked the whip lightly over the backs of the bays.

Millie kept quiet but inquired of herself "How did those folks and Miz Root git together? Ab must have my papers--my bound time ain't up yet. I ain't done nothing wrong--The Lord Himself knows that-- I guess I'll have to wait on the answer to this puzzle."

Her empty stomach and the team's accelerated pace over the uneven dirt road kept the girl wide awake. She began to recognize some landmarks in the growing light and when Abijah halted their horses to put out the lantern which had been their traveling light, she exclaimed "There's Halls' store! We're on the toll road now, ain't we? This here is Southville, Ab!"

Abijah admitted, "Ye're right again but best say Starkville, Millie. They've changed the name. We'll give the team a drink here at the waterin' trough, rest 'em a few minutes and be on our way."

They had been traveling on again a few minutes when Abijah, curious, asked "How did you know that was Starkville, Two-Bits?'

"I was bound out to Miz Root there," the girl replied. "My mother and I lived there for awhile. I got to know some of the folks. Miz Hall was always nice to me. She'd give me a sweet sometimes."

Ab made no comment but turned the team off the plank road, taking another dirt road that would ease them around the toll gate looming in the near distance and bring them down the high road into Fort Plain.

It was nearing seven when Abijah pulled the lathered team through the open doors of a sprawling livery stable in the center of the village of Fort Plain.

A man who was extinguishing lanterns hung about the dusky interior of the stable hurried over to offer his assistance.

"Let me help you down, young miss" he said politely to Millie and to Abijah "Rub your teams down, Mr. Abijah? And bait 'em?"

Abijah nodded and the man went bustling about his chores.

Seeing the astonished look on Millie's face, her companion laughed. "Never see'd a black man afore?" he whispered. "Pay no special mind. Wash wouldn't hurt a flea."

In a louder tone, he urged "Come now, let's get over to Daisy's kitchen. I promised you should eat and so you shall." As they crossed from the side door of the stable to the back door of the Hall, Ab took a small object from his vest pocket and thrust it into Millie's hand. "A thingumabob to remember your Uncle Ab by" he said hurriedly. "Jest don't go showin' it around, hear?"

CHAPTER 2

"Slow down, girl. There's plenty more where that came from. My land, you ain't nothing but skin and bone. Didn't they feed you up there?"

Millie stopped momentarily her assault on the ham and eggs and saleratus biscuits. "Yes, ma'am, only not quite so high on the hog."

Daisy Bogardus laughed heartily. She was a big-boned well-built woman, fairly tall, with kindly features and ever-ready smile. "Well, now, you speak plainly, Millie, and I like that. When you are ready, Molly will show you around and introduce you to our people."

While the cook was talking, a comely dark-haired girl came briskly into the room, carrying a broom and dustpan in one hand and a tray in the other.

"Here she is, now!" said Daisy. "Molly, this is Millie, our new girl. You two can get acquainted while you make the rounds. How's Miz Smith today?"

"About the same, Daisy. Complaining about her rheumatiz as usual. Funny thing, though. She asked me if the new girl was here yet."

"Well," Daisy said, "it beats me how she contrives to know ever'thing that's going on, but I got too much to do today to try to figure

it out! Be sure to take Millie in to
see her. That'll shorten her reins!"

As the two girls left the
kitchen, Molly said "I'm aiming to
show you over the whole building, all
three stories of it and you can meet
the Bowens when they come in and the
girls and a few others, but first,
what's your whole name, Millie?"

"Well, now, Pa named me
Millicent Evelina Cooper, but Ma said
that wuz too hi-falutin' for somebody
two bits short of a dollar, so I'm
just plain Millie."

"That explains what Abijah said
to Daisy whilst your back was turned
(I was in the pantry then, so I
overheard) but I'm not calling you
"two-bits"--where's your folks,
anyway?"

"Pa died 'bout seven years ago
and Ma up and run off with a
travelin' man after she bound me out.
Do you have folks, Molly?"

"Both dead with cholera, last
time it came through here. The
Bowens took me in and here I am,
although I plan to get married in the
fall. I'm 17 and walking out with
Johnny Dawley."

"My, this is a big place"
commented Millie as they started down
a long hall leading away from the
kitchen.

"It is that and it's the best
of the hotels in this fair village of
Fort Plain," said Molly proudly.
"Sure, there are ten others and not
one can hold a candle to Montgomery
Hall."

"But here, this is the public room, right here on the corner of Canal and Mohawk street. It's nice and big, as you can see, with enough tables and chairs and benches for a fair-sized crowd. The bar there, is for those who wish to have a nip, but you'd be surprised to see how many Fort Plainers just come in to gossip or play cards or sit around and exchange stories. The barkeep, Mr. High and Mighty himself, will be in at twelve o'clock, when the main traffic starts to come in."

As she saw Millie looking at her curiously, Molly explained "His real name is Livingston Van Alstyne, Millie. Short of Mr. Bowen, he's our official host and does his job very well. It's just that he's from one of the oldest families and never forgets it."

Motioning to two doors at the west end of the spacious room, Molly went on, "One opens into storage quarters and the other into a back entry which is convenient for deliveries and access to the livery stable on Mohawk Street. You must have seen 'Wash' Rayburn, the stablehand; but the boss out there is Julius Higgins and it's best to stay on his good side!"

"Isaiah, Daisy's husband, is jack-of-all-trades and helps out where and when needed. Doesn't talk much. Neither does Napoleon Jones, our night watchman and extra helper as needed. Our laundress is Lizzie Higgins and our seamstress is Johnny's mother, Elvira Dawley and that's usually the extent of our help. Mr. and Mrs. Bowen and Mary Eloise and Anna have their own chores. Mostly, we get along like one big family."

As Molly escorted her through the dining room, parlour and several smaller rooms on the first floor, "Two Bits" or Millie as she shall be called from now on, expressed appreciation and wonderment at the construction of the building.

"I want to say! Must hev been a fair bunch o' carpenter folk who put this up. Look'ee at that dainty 'scotten. Ain't it be-yootiful?"

Molly, albeit pleased, hastened to correct the other girl. "That's wainscoting, Millie. How do you come to call it 'scotten?"

"My Pa was a carpenter. I remember, though it was years back, him callin' it that."

"Well, Millie, it is beautiful as you say, but I'm honor bound you'll be having your turn at the polishing of it. Now, let's go up to the second floor."

The wide and deep oaken stairs that led up to the next floor received their share of Millie's admiration and Molly cried "I declare, I'm beginning to feel a bit jealous. I thought I was the only one who loved this place."

Seeing the hurt look on Millie's face, Molly hastily explained "I'm just teasing you, Millie. It is really nice to find someone else who appreciates good

workmanship. We hope the Hall will
be here for many a long year to
come."

When they stepped onto the
landing at the top of the stairs
Millie, looking first to the left and
then to the right, blurted out "It's
just as nice up here as down below.
My, it surely is elegant, the
woodworkin' and the fancy doors and
all. I wouldn't mind stayin' here
for good."

Molly laughed. "You'll be here
for awhile, anyway. It's my place
you'll be taking when I'm away this
fall. You'll get to know every one
of these rooms, what with making up
beds, delivering parcels and doing
endless cleaning and dusting.

Right now, you're going to meet
our permanent boarder, Mrs. Phidia
Smith."

She led the way to the end of
the hall and leaning past Millie,
knocked gently on the door, calling
out "Mrs. Smith, may we come in?"

The door opened so suddenly
that Millie nearly fell into the
room.

"Next time, knock a little
louder. I barely heard you,"
instructed the grey-haired woman who
had opened the door.

Molly, suppressing a giggle,
pushed the other girl ahead of her
into the center of the pleasantly
furnished room, saying "Mrs. Smith,
this is Millie Cooper, our new girl.
She'll be able to be of service to
you as soon as she learns how we do
things around here."

"Like as not she will. What's the matter, girl? Aren't you feeling well? Speak up!" The questions were addressed to Millie.

Millie shook her head vigorously. "No, ma'am. I mean, yes ma'am. That is, I'm all right., ma'am!"

"Well, well, better take her along, Molly. We can get better acquainted another time." Re-opening the door, Mrs. Smith ushered them out.

"I don't think we'll go up on the third floor today. You really do look a bit upset. Can you tell me what's troubling you?" asked Molly.

"I ain't so odd but what I know strange goin's on and that's all that's been happenin' this day. I think I know that lady, but disremember exactly how." Millie answered slowly.

"Tell me more," urged Molly; "but, sh'h'h, we'll get away from this door. We can start dusting in the other rooms. Let's go to the supply closet first and get you a cap and apron like I have. Are your things down in the kitchen?"

"I don't have much," confessed Millie. "What I got on, and a smidgin' more."

"Well, our seamstress can make up what you need and I'll lend you until she does, since we're about the same size. You'll be quartered with me, no doubt, and it will be nice to have someone to share things with. What's that just dropped out of your pocket?"

Millie hadn't yet seen what Ab had given her but now as she exchanged her dingy, patched apron for a fresh, snowy-white one, she saw a shiny thimble rolling across the floor.

Molly picked it up and exclaimed, "This is real silver, Millie. How did you come by it, if I may ask?"

So encouraged, and while the two girls began "redding up" the hotel's second floor rooms, Millie spilled out her puzzlement of the day's events.

Molly listened carefully and as they closed the door of the last room, she said "It's my thought, Millie, that you had better let sleeping dogs lie, as the saying goes; at least for awhile. And better heed Abijah's advice. Don't show your treasure around. Folks might get the wrong idea. For myself, I think you're going to be a great asset to Montgomery Hall and I hope we'll become fast friends."

CHAPTER 3

Downstairs once more and back in the kitchen, the girls found that Mr. and Mrs. Bowen had come in and were discussing their plans for the day with Daisy.

Millie found they were a kindly couple, pleasant in appearance and manner. Eve Bowen's hair was already showing quite a bit of grey, while Solomon was starting to lose his.

Eve Bowen interrupted her instructions to the cook to welcome Millie. "So you're our new helper; Millie Cooper, is it? We're glad you're here, because we have work enough today for all hands and then some!"

"Now then, Mother, don't scare the young lady off entirely. Millie, welcome to Montgomery Hall. I'm Solomon Bowen, the so-called boss around here, but don't you believe it! The ladies run the Hall, pure and simple. Howsomever, anything I can do to make you comfortable, just name it!" Mr. Bowen had a twinkle in his eye, but Millie felt instinctively that he was a force to be reckoned with.

"Now, Mother," he continued, "let's get out of here and go see Livingston. I heard him sashayin' around out in the taproom and I need to give him a line on today."

When they had gone, Daisy said half-seriously "As if there was anything Liv don't know already. Anyhow, this is what's afoot, girls. There's a sizable group of people coming in around four o' clock this afternoon--not on the train; being's this foreigner don't like trains, they're bringing their own spate of carriages. It's some kind of Eyetalian ambassador who wants to see the Mohawk Valley. Why he picked Fort Plain we'll never know, but it means all the rooms upstairs have to be done up special and finding space in the stables for two extra carriages and eight extra horses and my cooking's got to be the best!"

Molly bristled. "Your cooking's always the best, Daisy."

The older woman accepted the compliment matter-of-factly, saying "You're prejudiced, Molly. Anyway, the girls are coming in to help, Ike has gone to get Nap and I'm for Moore's Market right now. When I get back, we'll have a bite to eat." "You can put fresh linen on the beds, girls, and see if the commodes are fit. Ike hates that job, but I guess he's taken care of it. He's a good man, my Ike is, but I have to keep tellin' him it's honest work, not like horse stealin'! I'll send word to Lizzie to come and help out, too."

Taking down her bonnet and cape from their peg on the wall, Daisy picked up a large basket and swept out the back door of the kitchen, still talking; "I'll get Wash to go along and help lug the vittles home."

Molly commented "My, Daisy's certainly in a stew. Millie, your face is an open book. What now?"

"They don't steal horses here in this big village, do they?" objected the hill-girl.

"You goose! Sure, and it goes on all over the place---not from this livery stable, you can be sure, but sometimes after a good rig has left, we hear of its being made off with on the road. But, come on, let's see to the rooms and be finished before mid-day meal."

When they came back down the wide front stairs, Molly saw the other girl glance through the doorway to the right and said resignedly "Well, alright, seeing you're curious, might as well go meet Mr.Van Alstyne, sooner or later."

Millie saw that now there was a fresh covering of sawdust on the floor and the brass spittoons had been burnished to a soft glow. A young man stood behind the long mahogany bar industriously polishing glasses. As they came into the room, his eyes went first to Molly and then to Millie. Without waiting for introductions, he asked "Is this your sister, Miss Maguire?"

Flushing, Molly's composure deserted her and she replied hotly "Sure and indeed, what if she is? I'd be proud to call her that. But as 'tis , this is Miss Millicent Cooper. Millie, this is Mr. Livingston Van Alstyne of a small place called Nelliston, across the river.   Since Isaiah and Nap take good care of your domain, Mr. Van Alstyne, Millie will not intrude in your affairs, at all, at all."

Condescendingly, the young man commented "When she gets her dander up, see how her Irish blood surfaces. Are you related to the Cooperstown family, Miss Cooper?"

He obviously did not expect the answer he received.

"Yes, I am, Mr. Van Alstyne, although I'd be proud to be kin to Molly, here." She drawled the "Van", pronouncing it "Vain".

Livingston tried to regain his dignity by assuring her "No offense intended, Miss Cooper. I fancied there was a resemblance. My apologies, and if you would be so kind, Miss Molly, will you ask Isaiah to step in here for a moment?"

The girls fled down the hall toward the kitchen and once safely there, broke into gratified laughter.

"Sure, and did you ever put him in his place, Millie. And are you really related to the judge? Oh, this is rich. Wait until I tell Johnny!"

"What's this all about, Molly? And what can we do while you're telling me?"

Looking around the neat room, Molly's eyes fell upon the huge copper kettle standing on the fireplace hearth and she said, "Daisy has been wanting to give this a good scouring. Let's take it out back now and surprise her when she comes in."

They worked in silence for awhile; then Molly said "This is the way it is. Livingston doesn't like it that I'm going to marry Johnny Dawley. He thinks I should upgrade myself--that is, marry him, who is of the aristocracy (by his account) and get away from my Irish background. You see, Johnny's and my folks came from the old country when the Canal was going through. Our dads worked on it. Folks looked down on them and called them all sorts of ugly names, forgetting that their own forebears were also immigrants. Johnny's mother is a fine woman and a fine seamstress. Mrs. Bowen employs her quite often and treats her as an equal, as indeed she is. What Livingston doesn't know is that the Dawleys are descended from Irish kings, and indeed, my own family, the Maguires, were not exactly peasants. In this new country, though, Millie, 'tis not necessary to boast of pedigrees. A man need only to follow the Golden Rule; and pay his taxes", she added.

"Johnny is reading law with Attorney Simms here in Fort Plain and for myself, Mrs. Bowen has seen to it that I have as good an education as her own girls. Don't mind me asking, Millie, but can you read and write?"

Millie said slowly, "I never had no schoolin', Molly. Didn't speak up smart like the other young 'uns, either, so folks figured I was short on brains. Mebbee I am, but I'm beginnin' to think some kind o' wool has been pulled over my eyes, leastwise, up 'til now."

"That settles it, Millie. I'll ask Mary Eloise if she'll teach you to read and write. She's one of the Bowen girls and come to think of it, they should have been back by now. Something must have gone wrong-Mr. Higgins drove them to Canajoharie early this morning to pick up some lace we can't get here in Fort Plain right now. Levi Hirsch, the peddler who was here a few days back, didn't have any, either. They're fair particular, our girls are--and if they want Irish lace, that's what they intend to have! Well, we've scoured this kettle to a fare-thee-well, Millie, and I hear a ruckus going on. Here comes Wash; let's ask him to carry this back inside for us."

The black man was coming out the back door hurriedly but stopped short at sight of the girls.

"You'd better git in there, missies, and help calm down the womenfolk."

"What happened, Wash?" cried Molly, not forgetting the kettle, which she motioned for him to take.

"They was a hold-up this side o' Canajoharie, and the team was near stole and you better git the hull story from them," Wash responded, setting the kettle down just inside the kitchen door and retreating to the stables.

"Now, girls, you're safe and sound and that's what's important. Stop blubbering, Anna, and let Mary Eloise tell us what happened." Mrs. Bowen was speaking.

The stockier of the two young women seated by the long table gradually dried her tears and accepted the cup of tea Daisy had poured for her. The other girl, a slender blonde with blue eyes, glanced a bit scornfully at her sister and told her audience, now enlarged by Mr. Bowen, "There's not much to tell. Coming out of Canajoharie and right near the Happy Hollow road, we were stopped by a couple of masked men with guns. They took our purses, our purchases, and our team, but Mr. Higgins went after them with his own gun, aided by another driver who came up just in the nick of time. They brought back our horses and we came home. That's all there was to it."

Anna sobbed "That ain't all there is to it, Ma! They stole our lace and there ain't any more in Canajoharie!"

"You're alive," said Sol Bowen sternly, "and the team is safe. I must reward Julius."

"Go easy, father," said Mary Eloise. "The other driver helped and I believe Mr. Higgins could have driven a mite faster past those trees where the thieves were hiding."

"All's well that ends--- well, pretty well," Eve Bowen said dryly. "Let's eat and make ready for the ambassador and his, what's the word, Eloise?"

"Do you mean 'entourage', Mother?" her daughter asked.

"Good a word as any, I guess," agreed her mother. "Daisy, why not go get Ike? He likes to eat, too."

****

"I'd like to git a whiff o' night air, Molly, afore I bed down. Be back in two shakes of a lamb's tail."

Standing outside the back door, Millie heard voices coming from the stable. Curious, she moved across the alley into the shadow of the tall shrubbery along the barn.

"You sure made yourself look good, Jule; had a good notion to cross you up and take the team, anyway. If it weren't for better fish to fry, we prob'ly would have!"

"Now hold on there, Ame. Stick to the plan. You'll spoil everything yet with your loose jaw."

Millie stifled a gasp. 'Ame's' voice sounded like the one she had heard in Root's barn up on the hills. "They'll never find him," it had said.

"More to puzzle on," she mouthed silently and hurried back into the Hall.

"What's amiss, Millie? You look all flustered," asked Molly. "Let's get to bed--big day tomorrow, you know."

"Just thinkin' this day has been the most beatenest of my whole life, is all," Mille told her roommate and hopped into her side of the big featherbed.

The girls were roused from sound sleep early the next morning by a soft rap on their door. Daisy opened it slightly and called in "Be as quick as you can--big day today."

Molly grumbled a bit as she poured water into the wash basin. "That's all we'll have around here for awhile-big days! I wish these bigwigs from New York or Washington or Europe or wherever would stay home and not bother us!"

Millie, astonished at what she heard, protested "I reckon it's pure sociable on their part, Molly. I think it's real nice they want to visit Fort Plain. It's a grand place, what with Montgomery Hall here and all."

Molly relented. "You're right, Millie. I'm sorry I was so uncharitable. Besides, it's good business for the whole village as well as the Hall." Emptying the wash basin into the slop-jar, she filled it with clean water and said, "Here, you wash up now and we'll dress and go over to the kitchen. I smell buckwheat cakes and maple syrup."

Daisy was serving her husband and Wash and another man whom she introduced to Millie as Julius Higgins. A dark browed tall, thin man, he did not favorably impress Millie, but she said "how-de-do" quietly and sat down with Molly at the other end of the table.

While they all ate, Daisy imparted more news. "Some other

folks came in real late last night, 'bout midnight. The train had trouble comin' up from Albany; so our rooms are just about filled. Remind me, Ike, to have Sol tell Liv we have no vacancy."

"Gettin' kind o' ritzy, ain't you Daisy?" inquired Julius with a touch of sarcasm in his voice. "NO VACANCY!"

"This place is dignified," snapped the cook, "so we'll use dignified language; if you can manage it!"

Millie thought "Here's something else to ponder on. Looks like it ain't all sweetness and light here, either."

Higgins was again speaking. "Who all's the new people? We already got a congressman, an Eyetalian duke that don't like our trains and more horseflesh than we got room for out in the barn."

"Well, now, not that it's in your stall, Mr. Higgins, the congressman is leaving and the gentleman from overseas is a count, not a duke. There's a New York City reporter and his mother with her lady's maid and a business couple from the big city. Johnny Dawley met the train and brought 'em over. There's some dunnage for you and Wash to pick up, over at the station. And George Elliott's back in town." Daisy paused for a second and continued, "Oh, I nearly forgot! Miz Smith desires you to come up. She wants to arrange for a horse and carriage to drive out some day soon. Says the month of May is rushing on and she wants to catch some spring before it's gone."

"Wash," directed the stable boss, "You git on out to the barn and I'll skin up 'n see what the Widder Smith wants, before George blows in. Him and me don't allez see eye to eye."

They heard him stomping noisily up the back stairs leading off from the kitchen and Daisy sighed. "He's a good man with horses," she said, "but real crotchety with most humans. Now, girls, you had better set up the table in the dining room, for the guests will be coming down shortly for their breakfast. About 20 or so, I make it. George and Johnny will probably eat here, and Sol and Eve and the girls. Set a couple extra places, just in case."

"Daisy always sets an extra place in case the Lord drops in," Molly confided as they closed the kitchen door behind them, "and she tries to keep one room empty, too."

"She is an awful good woman, seems like," the other girl commented. "Ain't she got any children?"

"She and Ike had three, but lost them all to the choking disease. She feels for young ones and I see she's taking an interest in you, Millie."

"That's real good to know, Molly. Now, how do we rig up the table? Where I lived, we et in the kitchen." Millie self-consciously adjusted her new cap and smoothed down her spotless apron, as she spoke.

When the guests assembled for breakfast, a self-assured handsome young woman detached herself from the group and headed for the kitchen. "I'm Rosina Myers, Mrs. Hearst's personal maid and I'm to eat out here," she announced; "I eat most anything, so don't go to any extra bother."

"Don't worry," Daisy replied comfortably, "You'll eat what the rest of us eat. Griddle cakes and maple syrup and sausage is on the menu for today's breakfast; tea or coffee, your choice and help yourself, because I have to see things go smooth in the dining room."

Daisy had put on a fresh outfit herself and now moved to the doorway of the dining room to supervise he girls and incidentally to get a peek at a real member of the Italian nobility. Convinced that everything was indeed proceeding properly, she came back and sat down beside the autocratic Miss Myers, inquiring "How do you find the food, Miss Rosina?"

"It's really quite good, but I believe a little coarse for Mrs. Hearst's delicate system. And I imagine Mr. ad Mrs. Biermann are unaccustomed to such heavy fare, also."

"Let 'em speak for themselves, Miss Rosina. If they're going to be here for two weeks, as I've been told, they'll get used to it, I'll be bound." Daisy was sparing in her sympathy.

The maid refused to be diverted from her criticism. "They may not stay that long--they've already been upset by the absence of Mr. Biermann's kinsman."

"Who would that be, Miss Rosina," asked Daisy.

"Mr. Hirsch, who came upstate about two weeks ago. He arranged to be here when the Biermanns arrived. They intend to start in business here, I understand. Mr. Biermann's brought a considerable amount of stock with him."

"You're talking about Levi, the peddler?" asked Daisy.

"Traveling merchant is so much nicer a term, don't you think? But yes, I mean Mr. Levi Hirsch. Has he been here?"

Before Daisy could answer, Molly and Millie came in, carrying trays stacked with plates to be washed, whereupon the cook asked "Molly, when was Levi here? Here's somebody needs to know."

Molly set her load down and thinking out loud, reported "Six days ago, maybe seven. Johnny and his mother were here and we were all looking at his goods, remember? Johnny got his mother a silver thimble--oh!" She stopped abruptly.

"Well, he ought to be back soon," advised Daisy. "He never reserves his room for more than two weeks."

****

An hour earlier, Phidia Smith had raked Julius Higgins over the coals, verbally. "If I had known Ernie Smith was a cousin of yours, I never would have married him. Well, that's water over the dam now; he's dead and well out of it. I saw your signal in the barn window and asked to have you come up, though it goes against the grain. What is it you're up to and where do I fit in?"

"Simmer down, Widder Smith. You know your plush quarters here are

for keepin' your mouth shut. Rhody
would have it that way; her and her
big heart! The thing of it now is,
Twobits may be catchin' on to the
operation, 'specially after the other
night. It was an accident, but..."

"Hah! Since when is robbery an
accident?" Phidia interrupted,
"Why'd you bring her down here; ahead
of time, at that. Her contract with
Neva isn't up till the end of the
month."

"Lorenzo's wife is soft in the
head, too," Julius replied
disgustedly. "Neva figured Millie'd
end up in the Otsquago, somewhere's,
if she stayed there. Besides, the
girl's your niece, ain't she, even if
she don't know it? You can figure
some way to keep her from talkin',
and if you want to keep on havin'
your bed and board scot-free, you'll
keep a muzzle on her."

****

The Count of Malamocco, attired
in morningwear and seated in a
comfortable upholstered chair in the
parlour of Montgomery Hall, was
outlining his plans for the next two
weeks. Audolph Hearst, assigned by
his newspaper, The Daily Sun, to
cover the ambassador's visit to the
Valley, was listening intently.
George Elliott was listening with one
ear, the other being attuned to the
light footstep of Mary Eloise Bowen,
should it occur.

"And other than viewing your
most beautiful countryside, I had
thought possibly to locate
descendants of my father's family,
the Alberti's. Two hundred years
ago, a younger son took employment on
a Lowlands trading vessel "The King

David," and sailed to your country. This was in our own port of Venice. He never returned. We have been able to ascertain that he changed his name slightly and that some of his family later came to this Mohawk Valley, which course of action I cannot fault, it is so peaceful here. In talking with your people, I hoped to narrow my search--" he flung out his arms, palms upturned, "otherwise, lo finite, end of search."

"Nevertheless, your Excellency, we shall try to assist you. Along the way, I may find a relative of my own who appears to be among the missing."

George's full attention swiveled to Audolph. "Who's lost? he demanded. "What's the story?"

Dolph laughed. "There speaks another journalist, your Excellency. George has it in mind to become a professional newsman, himself." He went on to explain about the plans of the Biermanns and Levi Hirsch, adding "He really is a cousin of sorts, of mine. Good old Levi, always did have a wandering foot. Honest as the day is long, though, and knows his stock in trade."

"We'll come across him out in the country, Dolph, haggling with a housewife over some article's caught her eye. Excuse me, gentlemen, for a few minutes. I'll be back shortly and we can get started on our investigations." And George departed in the direction of the kitchen.

CHAPTER 5

Nearly a week passed with no clue as to Levi's whereabouts. Discouraged and apprehensive, the ladies and gentlemen of Montgomery Hall met again in the parlour to discuss their next step.

The count by now had given up his own quest and was eagerly supporting the search for the missing peddler. "I would like to meet this good man," he told the group, "for we have found no one with a bad word for him, and this is a most unusual circumstance."

Mrs. Bowen added her own commendation. "Levi is an honest peddler, that is," with an apologetic glance at Miss Myers, "traveling merchant." That young lady, seated beside Mrs. Hearst, nodded graciously. At the moment, she was engaged in offering her employer, who was on the verge of tears, a voluminous white handkerchief.

"Always pays his room rent in advance," Mrs. Bowen continued, "two weeks always, no more, no less."

"Did he give anyone his itinerary?" Dolph asked, with notebook in hand and pencil poised.

"Not unless it was to Julius, who would naturally want to know where Mr. Bowen's favorite driving mare was going. Sometimes Levi stayed overnight when his route was lengthy, like up along the Otsquago and over on the Squak." George Elliott volunteered this information.

"Once in a while I've gone along with him on a short route. Wanted to try my hand at some kind of story, Dolph. Story or not, it was interesting. He could pull more stuff out of his boxes and bags: tinware, clocks, tools, needles, thimbles, thread, jewelry and all kinds of lace and ribbon and bolts of cloth. Always had something for each child and didn't charge a cent for that. Remember that baby with the fancy rattle, over on the Pike? I'll wager he got it from Levi!"

"Something I didn't cotton to, George, was what a few folks suggested--had we considered the Swamp Gang? From what you've told me, maybe we had better do just that," said Dolph, "although I hate to think what it might mean."

"May I suggest, gentlemen," Johnny Dawley spoke up now, "perhaps there should be put a guard on the hotel stables, since the Ambassador has two fine four-in-hands out there? The Swamp Gang has its informers. Also I've heard they can change the appearance of any horse by various means, even using hot potatoes to make white markings where there were none before, and paint to cover existing colors so rightful owners would not recognize their property."

Millie, sitting in the corner next to the kitchen door, stiffened and Molly, standing beside Johnny on the other side of the door, noticed. "Stay later," she whispered to her intended.

It was close on to nine o'clock the next morning when Mrs. Bowen came into the kitchen and crossed over to the table where Johnny sat in earnest conversation with Molly and Millie. She said "I hate to interrupt your conference, but we do have to get on with the regular chores, girls, and John, don't you think Mr. Simms might be wondering where you are?"

"I'm on my way, Mrs. Bowen, but perhaps later you would let the girls fill you in on what we've been discussing. And Mr. Simms is going to learn about this too." Picking up his cap, Johnny left by the side-door, whistling cheerfully.

"Is this lawyer business, Molly?" inquired Eve Bowen with a skeptical look on her face.

"It's about Mr. Hirsch, Mrs. Bowen. Johnny is gathering evidence about a possible crime, he says," the girl replied, "and Millie may be a witness--" She stopped talking, noticing that Julius had come in while she was speaking.

"Is Sol around, ma'am?" he asked.

"I believe he is with Livingston in the taproom, Julius. Go right in."

The stablemaster went down the hall and Molly whispered "Do you think he heard me?"

Eve Bowen advised "If you stop talking and go on up to start on the rooms, you needn't worry about anybody listening."

She was wrong. Julius had heard and Millie was in real jeopardy from that moment. To make matters worse, while he was consulting with Sol Bowen, a messenger came in with a note from Attorney Simms, requesting Sol to come to the office as soon as possible.

"We'll straighten out this

matter as soon as I get back, Julius," Sol told his stablemaster, "for now, things stay as they are."

"Yes, sir," Julius looked none too pleased as he left the room.

"It may not be my place to advise, Mr. Bowen," said Livingston, as he held up the glass he was polishing, "but I should be careful in dealing with Mr. Higgins, if I were you."

"Liv, as usual, you have hit the nail squarely on the head. Please let Mrs. Bowen know where I am," and Solomon opened the big doors of the public room to descend the front steps with a firm, measured tread.

A man who appreciated his village and his neighbors, Solomon passed slowly down Canal Street, surveying with satisfaction the improvements that had come about since the Great Fire of '55. Brick buildings had taken the place of the wooden ones destroyed in the fire, mostly on Main Street up ahead, but some on Canal and new businesses were coming in at a good rate. "I hope the Biermanns stay," he mused; "We need a general merchandise emporium capacious enough to attract trade from all over the valley. We've got a nice school up on the hill, the Canal goes right through town and the railroad's just across the bridge. We're right up to date, counting the wireless, as any community could be. I hope the war some are predicting between the states never comes to pass. We need our young men."

He had reached 7 Canal Street by now and stepped in through the open door, being greeted by Johnny, who promptly went to call his employer from the coffee shop next door.

"Well, well, you certainly are prompt, Solomon. How's the family today?" Without waiting for a reply the bustling, ruddy-cheeked little lawyer led the way to a corner farthest from the door where his desk stood, piled high with papers. He motioned for Johnny to join them. "I trust the chairs are comfortable; bought 'em over at the Hix place. They're branching out into furniture now. Fort Plain's getting to be a real industrial town, for sure. Now, to business. John informs me of a potential criminal case, which is intriguing, but nebulous. However, from what he tells me, I can see that you and the Hall might easily become involved; innocently, I'm sure; ergo, your presence here. John can tell you what he has learned so far in connection with the disappearance of Mr. Levi Hirsch. John--?"

"Well, Mr. Bowen, this is how it stands. Audolph Hearst, a relative of Levi, has retained Mr. Simms as counselor and official investigator in the case. This last office he has kindly delegated to me and I have determined these facts:

Mr. Hirsch rented his usual room at your hotel two weeks ago and arranged for a horse and carriage to make his regular trips into the surrounding countryside.

From inquiries made subsequently, it seems he was last observed in the Squak area above Van Horne's Mills. We have not been able to pinpoint his final call, but plan to re-visit that neighborhood to do some in-depth questioning.

Miss Cooper has informed us of certain activities which may have a bearing on the case. It is my understanding that your stablemaster rented a valuable horse to Mr. Hirsch?"

"My best driving mare," Mr. Bowen assented. "She was the only beast left in the barn that morning. My word, Joseph, you have a legal eagle here!"

Joe Simms smiled proudly and Johnny, blushing modestly, continued. "Mr. Elliott tells us that the gang of horse thieves operating out of a county west of us is adept at changing the looks of an animal so as to safely sell it without detection; among other tricks, applying hot potatoes to form a white patch where desired.

Miss Cooper lived as a bound servant in one home up there and says that the peddler, that is, Mr. Hirsch, showed his goods to the household one evening and was offered lodging for the night. Extremely early the next morning, Miss Cooper was roused from bed and given a kettle of hot potatoes to take to the barn. Upon her return to the house a few minutes later, she was rushed off, without explanation, to Montgomery Hall here in Fort Plain. She says it was very dark in the barn on the hill, with one small lantern only, but she heard a man's voice bragging "He'll never be found, so don't worry."

Miss Cooper is certain she heard this same voice coming from your stable that same evening, when she had stepped outside the kitchen for a breath of fresh air before retiring. It is fairly certain, or rather, we must assume that someone in your employ is implicated.

George tells us that you have at times lost valuable animals; not directly from your livery barn, but when they were out on rental. Would you confirm this, Mr. Bowen?"

"I'd give a pretty penny to catch the thieves," Sol growled, "but I'm not the only one who suffers loss. We're about ready to form an Association. Enough's enough!"

Johnny continued his report: "Since we don't yet know the scope of the situation, Mr. Simms feels it may be advisable for you to arrange for some kind of protection for your stables and of course, for Miss Cooper, taking as few persons into your confidence as possible.

The Ambassador's men are currently attending the stable since his stock is blooded and quite valuable. We welcome your suggestions, Mr. Bowen. Remember, it is well-known that this gang will stop at nothing to gain their ends."

"I think I can round up some help," Sol agreed. "They might's well be doing something instead of cluttering up the bar-room. I'll see about it directly I get back to the Hall. I'll keep it under my hat as best I can."

"You might let Liv in on the situation," Johnny said. "He's got a keen eye."

As Sol turned to go, Johnny said "Just one more thing, come to think of it, Mr. Bowen. What do you know about your boarder, Mrs. Smith? It seems Julius is more or less at her beck and call, Daisy tells me."

"Well, now, John, she pays her tab regularly and that has to count with me," Solomon responded. Wrinkling his brow, he commented "Seems to me it might be 'tother way around with her and Julius, but then, again, I don't rightly know. Keeps to herself, mostly. Drives out, once in a while; has Molly get her necessaries. Been with us six, maybe seven years. You could ask Eve or better yet, Molly." Similing, Sol continued, "I know you and Molly have plans for this fall but I hope this matter is cleared up before then, so you and she will have only personal matters to attend to, then. The girls will be sending to see what's become of me, so I bid you gentlemen good day."

When he had gone, Joseph Simms raised an eyebrow quizically and remarked, "We'll be losing you to Pinkerton's Agency, one of these days, no doubt?"

John blushed, but reassured his mentor: "Fort Plain is an up and coming community, sir, and I intend to help it grow."

CHAPTER 6

"Julius, you've got to quit coming up here so often. Somebody's going to get suspicious."

"Suspicious of what, Widow Smith? Nobody'd be courtin' you, that's for sure. I have my orders to pass on to you and that's that," Julius replied arrogantly.

"Well, you sure know one thing and that's how to hurt a body. As far as your orders go, I haven't yet been able to get Millie alone for any length of time to talk with her and find out what she knows or doesn't know. She and Molly usually work together cleaning my room and I don't aim to get Molly in Dutch. She's a jewel of a girl and as far as that goes, I'm finding Millie is cut out of the same cloth. You say they want her back on the hill? Why? So she can disappear like Levi?" Phidia was highly indignant.

She went on, asking "Where is everybody this afternoon? No one answered my bell."

"Calm down, woman. The girls are out doing errands for Eve, and the Bowens, all four of 'em, are down at Keller & Walrath's gettin' Sol all gussied up with a new suit for the big doin's."

"What big doings?" demanded Phidia.

"Got ahead of you there, didn't I?" taunted Julius. "There's gonna be a Grand Ball on account of that Eyetalian duke bein' here; and I reckon it'll be an engagement party

for George and Mary Eloise, too. I
hear he brought a ring up from the
city. I hear he's wrote a real nice
poem for his ladylove, in the
bargain, so we'll prob'ly get to hear
that, too. I guess Lizzie slipped up
there, not lettin' you in on it."

"I don't depend on her for all
the news," Phidia snapped back. "And
you better skedaddle now. Just get
this straight: orders or no orders,
I'm waiting 'til after this Grand
Ball has come and gone!"

"I'll let you know what's
decided on," Julius replied
imperturbably and glided discreetly
from the room.

A troubled Mrs. Smith sank back
in her chair. "I can't let them take
Millie back to that den of iniquity,"
she thought, as she realized Julius
hadn't answered her questions. Too,
why hadn't Lizzie come today to get
her laundry? "I should have asked
Julius where his sister was," Phidia
decided, thinking "I mistrust what's
afoot."

****

Eve Bowen had decreed that the
Grand Ball would best take place on
the last Saturday of the month. That
would allow time for preparation by
the Hall as well as by the village,
for she envisioned a community
festival, as indeed it turned out to
be.

At the Hall, Eve issued
commands like a seasoned General. To
Lizzie Higgins, she instructed "Find
a couple of ladies to help you clean
the ballroom thoroughly. Pay special
attention to the windows. I want
them to sparkle like diamonds. I'm
glad we chose the plum drapes, aren't

you, Elvira?" addressing this question to Johnny's mother, who stood with scissors in hand at the long dining room table, which was loaded with fabrics and laces and other stuffs.

"The girls can tell you what they want," Eve went on. "You already know what I intend to wear. You can make your own hours and go right to work now, if you can." She added "Eloise and Anna will help you when they have finished with the invitations."

"Mama, what about Molly ad Millie? Shouldn't they have new gowns, too?" asked the considerate Eloise.

"Why, I had thought they would be serving---." Eve paused only briefly and said energetically "Of course they shall have new dresses. We'll have the Greene girls come in to serve. You can contact them, Eloise."

Eve was not yet finished with the sewing arrangements. "Anna, I want you should go up and ask the ladies if they require any sewing done. Make a list and give it to Elvira, please, my dear. Thank you. I'll ask George to consult with the gentlemen on their needs. Where is George today, anyway, Eloise?" she concluded.

Together with Dolph Hearst and the Count, George had gone to the hill country above Van Horne's Mills, Eloise informed her. "Daisy prepared a lunch for them and they'll probably have a marvelous day. I only wish I could have gone along, too!"

"All in good time, my girl," Eve advised. "Wait'll you and George are married. He'll probably drag you all over creation, chasing down one of his 'stories'."

"Mama, George wants to be a good reporter, like Dolph, and maybe even have his own newspaper some day." Eloise defended her absent lover.

"Well, well, we won't argue about it, dear. I hope he's getting a good story today," her mother said soothingly.

****

Out on the hills, the Count was enjoying himself hugely. The day was warm, but not oppressively so, and the blue sky and spring air conspired to make him wax poetic; in Italian, much to George's disappointment. As they traversed the steep hills, George asked if he could read some verses he himself had composed while coming up on the train from New York City.

Dolph questioned in an amused manner "When did you find time to do that? I didn't notice any writing going on."

"Dolph, you can't notice anything when you're sleeping."

Here the Count intervened diplomatically, saying he himself would like very much to hear the verses.

"Well, then," George reddened a bit, "here goes!"

"Bonnie Eloise,
the Belle of the Mohawk Vale"

"O, sweet is the vale where the Mohawk gently glides
On its clear winding way to the sea-
And dearer than all storied streams

on earth besides
Is this bright rolling river to me-
Chorus:
But sweeter, dearer, yes, dearer
far than these
Who charms where others all fail,
Is blue-eyed, Bonnie, Bonnie Eloise,
The Belle of the Mohawk Vale."

"There's more," George said, "but here we are at the Lorenzo Root farmhouse. We did want to stop here, didn't we?"

Dolph nodded. "I wasn't real happy with the answers we got when we were here before."

****

In the law office at 7 Canal Street in Fort Plain, Joe Simms was giving his young assistant carte blanche in the matter of the Levi Hirsch case. "Take all the time you need, John, up to two weeks, anyway. Try to wind it up by the end of the month--just abou the time of the Great Ball I'm hearing so much about from my wife!"

"Yes sir, Mr. Simms, and thank you for giving me a free hand, so to speak. You've been like a real dad to me since my own died." Johnny's eyes misted over.

"Well, well, no need to get sentimental, my boy. Your father was a good man and I can see that you're a chip off the old block, as they say. The Canal has brought us many benefits, but it took its toll, and still does, for that matter. The constable fished another corpse out of the waters early this morning. So far, no identification.

"Well, go ahead, John. I know you're champing at the bit. Touch base once in a while, won't you?" and the older man, with an affectionate smile lighting up his usually solemn countenance, shooed Johnny out the door.

****

The coming Grand Ball was having a salutary effect on the whole village. Enthusiasm begets enthusiasm. Anxious to share in any boom, however temporary, shopkeepers brightened up displays and instituted entire new ones. Milliners and seamstresses shook out folds of latest fabrics while explaining the very newest styles from New York and London to prospective patrons. Windows were given in-between scheduled washings and streets swept clear of the trash which had accumulated. Contents of flower beds were viewed with an eye to up-coming decoration. In short, Fort Plain was on its toes and rarin' to go.

A teller at the bank was grumbling one morning "Can't see what all the fuss is about--haven't had my coffee break yet this morning, so much money coming in and the foyer cluttered up with people talking their heads off!"

His fellow bank servant, sitting on the stool next to him, remonstrated, "Henry, they ought to do this more often--it's good for the town and business--hello! What's this? Call the president, Henry. I think we've got a counterfeit note here, on the Oneida Bank. Now, who could have turned this in?"

****

Before continuing on to the Hall, Johnny had stopped at the

undertaker's and at the end of his brief visit, thoroughly agreed with that worthy's opinion: "Ain't no tellin' who he was--time and the weather--his own mother wouldn't know him. So I can't answer your question, Johnny."

****

"No sir, like I told you before, Levi hasn't been here this time around." Neva Root absent-mindedly fingered the brooch she was wearing and continued, "Now, gentlemen, I'm cleaning house and if you'll excuse me, I'd like to get on with it." She closed the door abruptly, terminating the conversation.

"That takes care of that," George said as they descended the porch steps and started back to their carriage. "But the neighbors said he'd been at their place."

"They live over a mile down the road, George, and a lot can happen in a mile. I'd like to talk with Mr. Root, but he never seems to be around," Dolph countered. "Who runs the farm?"

"Abijah Smith sees to it, I believe," George replied. "He supplies the Hall with eggs, beef and sometimes mutton. We might ask him some questions."

The Count, who had kept silent until now, commented "I see the lady has impeccable taste, as evidence the brooch she was wearing. An excellent copy of an Italian original--Medici, I believe."

Dolph and George stared at each other.

"Mother has one just like it! why didn't I remember that?" cried

Dolph. "Levi gave it to her the day before he left the city. Said he was bringing a few up to Fort Plain for the store."

George, ever pragmatic, asked "What do we do now?"

The Count, again displaying true diplomacy, offered "Georgio, I would like to hear the rest of your so beautiful poem!"

CHAPTER 7

"Now here's the plan, Phidia. Listen careful and make no mistake. Your life depends on it.

Ame says we should plan to pick up Millie the morning after the big shindig; folks'll be too groggy to know what's goin' on. You'll take the girl out for a sightseein' ride up Sand Hill way. Tell her that's where Fort Plain used to be, or something like that. You've got the gift o' gab. Ame 'n another feller and me will do the rest."

"Julius, you've got a cruel heart--why do they want her back? She's just begun to fit in here and have a decent home life. She won't make trouble. Can't they leave her alone?"

"Now, Phidia, we know she's been talkin' to Molly and that young whippersnapper of a lawyer, and now he's pokin' around askin' questions about the peddler. Not only that, but he's got George and that big city newspaper man in on it. Ame don't want no witnesses to tell no tales. Just do as you're told and no harm'll come to you, Phidia."

Phidia made no comment; merely opened the door of her room and motioned for the stablemaster to leave.

"Lizzie does her own reporting well," she thought bitterly. "She's probably following the girls around right now."

****

The evening of the Grand Ball

- 44 -

had arrived. The weather had cooperated and the village was bathed in the soft afterglow of a colorful sunset. "Titian," murmured the Count as he was being assisted to dress in full ambassadorial regalia by his valet.

Signore Guglielmo Fabriano, who was also his secretary, smiled to see his employer so full of good fellowship. "Perhaps he will take this democratic attitude home," Guglielmo thought. "Imagine! The drivers and footmen being bidden to the ball (they had also been eating at table with His Excellency), even as he himself (William, as he thought of himself now) would be attending. The grandeur of this occasion promised to equal or even surpass similar events at home in Malamocco, the capital of Venezia, which was itself the trading capital of the world.

Magnifico! Moreover, reverting to more prosaic considerations, having such a good command of this uncouth language, he might be able to become better acquainted with the personable, albeit reserved Miss Rosina Myers.

True, he and the others had been detailed to help watch for trouble that night, but taking turns, it wouldn't be too hard to get in some merrymaking as well.

For some that evening, there was more than merrymaking on their minds and in their hearts.

When Phidia Smith had closed the door on Julius three days before the Ball, she had for the first time in years sought the help of her Maker. "Dear God in Heaven," she

prayed earnestly, "help me get Millie
out of this mess and I'll do all I
can to make amends for what I've done
wrong."

She remained on her knees a
long time, then got up and resolutely
went out her door. She saw no one in
the wide paneled hallway and so
quickly scurried across to Mrs.
Hearst's room, tapping softly and
repeatedly.

Sarah Hearst opened the door
with a questioning look on her gentle
motherly face. "You must be Mrs.
Smith," she said. "Come in. What
can I do for you?"

Phidia entered, looking around
cautiously. "It's confidential," she
said. "Are we alone?"

"Oh yes. Rosina's out shopping
with Mrs. Biermann. Do sit down and
tell me what's troubling you, for I
do see trouble on your face. Shall I
ring for tea?"

"No, no," Phidia replied
hurriedly. "No one must know I've
spoken with you. This is why I'm
here---" Quickly, she told Sarah
Hearst about Millie, the plot to
kidnap her and the fact that this
might lead to her niece's death.
"I'm not proud of my part in this and
I don't know where to turn for help.
I thought your son, being a
newspaperman, might be able to come
up with something. I hear he's a
mighty smart young man. What I
really hope for is to get my niece
out of this area to a safe place far
enough away so's the Swamp Gang won't
ever find her."

"Well," said Sarah, and
Phidia's heart warmed to the other
woman's obvious sympathy, "we have

all of three days and this should be sufficient for Dolph to come up with a counterplot. Be of good cheer, Phidia. May I call you that? I do think we'll have to have a few more collaborators, though; maybe Molly and George and probably that bright young man of Molly's, John Dawley. We'll have their promise to keep it under their hats, of course. My, I came up for a rest, but this is most exciting, so who wants to rest? I'll have to manage to keep this from Rosina. Now, best scoot back to your room before she comes back. I'll let you know as soon as Dolph comes up with something."

Now three days later on the eve of the ball, Dolph and Johnny and Molly were putting the finishing touches on their plan to foil the kidnappers.

"Molly told Millie this afternoon, Dolph," Johnny said, "and she took our plan very well. There is a real smart young lady."

"Yes, she is, and I'm proud of her," Molly concurred. "I'm going to miss---"

"Sh'h, someone's coming," warned Johnny. "But let Liv in on the details, will you, Dolph? I'll tell you why, later."

Isaiah came into the storeroom where the three conspirators stood talking. "Jest need a couple more lanterns to hang where the street lights don't reach," he explained. "My sakes, never see'd so many people out and about after sundown." He picked the lanterns off a shelf and left.

The three left also, Dolph to go out to the taproom and Molly and

Johnny to ascend the polished oaken stairs to the second floor, where they proceeded to Mrs. Smith's door. When she opened it, they slipped in quickly.

"Everything's arranged, Mrs. Smith," Johnny said. "I expect Mrs. Hearst has given you the details. May God be with you tomorrow."

"I wish you were going upstairs with us," Molly coaxed. "It's going to be such a gala evening."

"I'll hear the band and that's enough," Phidia said and smiled. "My, you young folks look lovely' and Millie, is she---?" Molly reassured her. "Millie looks grand, Mrs. Smith. I taught her how to dance and Liv is escorting her. With her new pink gown and all, she'll remember this night all her life!" And Molly impulsively kissed the cheek of the older woman, down which tears were beginning to slide.

As they climbed the last flight of stairs leading to the ballroom, Johnny sighed and putting his arm around her, said "Molly dear, I wish tomorrow were over!"

CHAPTER 8

From the bushes outside the east wall of the stable came a loud whisper. "Antonio, it has been some time since Signore Wash or Signore Napoleon came out to tell us all is well."

"Vincenzo, you are right. Let us enter this door quietly and investigate." Antonio thereupon held the door sufficiently open for his fellow guardsman to slide through.

Vincenzo flashed him a quizzical look, but went in noiselessly. When Antonio followed, he saw Vince tapping someone on the shoulder and heard him say "Scusi, signore." As the man turned, Vincenzo's fist shot out and Antonio stepped gracefully forward to receive the intruder as he fell.

"Signore Wash, are you alright?" asked Vincenzo as he brushed the stablehand off and released him from his bonds and gag.

"I'm jes' fine, sir, but let's see if Nap is alright, too. He's over by the fine gentleman's horses, or should be, sir. There's another one of them scalawags about, so be careful, sir."

"I trust the horses are alright," Antonio remarked. "They are French Demi Sang animals and very valuable."

The carriage horses were found in fine fettle, chewing quietly on the hay before them in their mangers. Nap was found bound and gagged between the last stall and a window, which was half-open. Freeing him, they closed the apparent getaway route of the other intruder and hurried back to the first one, only to find him gone. "Flew the coop, I guess," was Nap's only assessment of the affair. "I'm goin' in and get a drink!"

"an excellent suggestion," agreed Antonio.

"Although we will join you when our replacements arrive," Vincenzo ended the proposition.

****

Upstairs in the ballroom of Montgomery Hall, Mr. and Mrs. Bowen were thoroughly enjoying the evening. They sat in specially cushioned chairs not too near the bandstand, since Sol had said previously he had no intention of having his eardrums 'busted.' Eve had led off the Grand March with the Count and danced one quadrille with her husband. There-after, she only desired to sit and listen to the music and watch the dancers and take note of all the beautiful gowns worn by the elite f the village. The Count and his staff were accomplished dancers, exciting the admiration and envy of the local belles and beaux. But Eve was glad to see that George and Eloise and even Anna and "Doc" Taylor were main-taining laurels for their hometown.

Sol echoed her thoughts when he said with a touch of pride in his voice, "Mrs. Bowen, it may be many a long year before such a sight is seen again in Fort Plain. People are purely enjoying themselves and no trouble, at least, not yet. Constable tells me he has put on a dozen extra men and they're circulatin' through the crowd down there, just in case. With the street dancin' and all, I don't reckon folks'll have mischief on their minds."

Eve interrupted him gently: "I think Dolph is going to say a few words now, while the band is having some refreshments, so let's listen."

Audolph Hearst did not make a long speech, merely related how much the Ambassador had appreciated the hospitality of the Valley and Fort Plain in particular and would carry home many pleasant memories of his visit. He had received a wireless message late this afternoon and would be leaving early in the morning, so he wished to express his thanks tonight. He paid tribute to his host and hostess, Dolph relayed, and complimented the comfort and beauty of Montgomery Hall. Dolph said he guessed that was all, but he himself had learned all over again how much the city was dependent on its country cousins.

"Sounds like a politician," Sol whispered to Eve.

The Count himself bowed low to the audience and expressed his emotional farewell in Italian, after which the highlight of the evening became apparent.

A blossom covered bower had been set up between two of the gleaming windows looking down on Canal Street and to this pretty nook, George Elliott led Mary Eloise. Her father thereupon arose from his chair and walking slowly across the floor to the flowered arch, took his daughter's hands and placed them in George's. The watching throng of dancers hushed to hear him say "Mrs. Bowen and I are pleased to announce the engagement of our daughter Mary Eloise to Mr. George Elliott and to wish them all happiness."

As a flurry of clapping and good wishes broke out, Sol held up his hand for silence and went on to say "Folks, George has a little engagement gift for our Eloise. He has written a poem in her honor and I think you might like to hear it. George, I believe you might just have it handy?"

George pulled it out of his pocket somewhat sheepishly and began to read.

Sol tiptoed back to his wife's side, whispering as he sat down, "Did I do alright?"

Giving his hand a surreptitious squeeze, Eve replied, "Of course, silly. You always do right. Well, nearly always."

The soft lamplight shed its beneficence over the swaying dancers, silken gowns twinkled across he floor on the arms of sartorially elegant male companions while the heady fragrance of lilacs and early roses drifted hither and yon from the open windows, and the band played on to the wee hours of the morning.

Montgomery Hall basked in the reflected glow of village hospitality. Seemingly, all was right with the world.

CHAPTER 9

Few inhabitants of Fort Plain were astir when the early morning sun peeped over the horizon on Sunday. Few, that is, except at Montgomery Hall where all was bustle and hurry.

Liv was restoring order to the public room, with a sleepy Napoleon Jones assisting.

Molly and Millie were serving breakfast in the dining room to the Count and his staff and to Dolph, his mother and Miss Myers, all of whom would depart shortly.

In the kitchen, Daisy was feeding the Hall crew; Julius, Wash and Ike and she was as usual, announcing the day's schedule. "His Excellency must leave as soon as possible, Julius, in order to make connections with the boat leaving for Venice, so as soon as you're finished, look to the luggage and the carriages, will you? I'm sure the Count's men will help, and Wash, too. What's wrong, Wash? Got a headache?"

"No, Ma'am," Wash tactfully replied, "jest a leetle bit too much, last night."

"Ike, you fix that cloth around Wash's head a mite tighter. Wash, let that be a lesson to you," the cook instructed. Continuing, Daisy reported "Mr. Hearst is taking his mother back to New York on the ten o'clock eastbound train. She's not feeling well and wants to get back to her own physician, though I told her our Dr. Snyder could probably fix her up."

Miss Myers, who had eaten in the dining room to be near her employer (though she was discomfited by this breach of protocol) came in while Daisy was speaking and with newly acquired tact, commented "Undoubtedly, Mrs. Bogardus, but Audolph must report to his editor. I'm glad that Miss Maguire is going as far as Albany to help with Mrs. Hearst in case she has one of her attacks before we make connections with the New York train."

"How's Molly gittin' back, Daisy?" inquired her taciturn mate.

"Joe Simms and his wife are going in to deliver some legal papers to a lawyer down there, Ike. I guess that answers your question. Anyhow, you know what needs to be done once this lot has checked out."

Ike subsided, his brief excursion into speech effectively cut short by the reminder.

Daisy went on "Now then, I guess that's all, except after we get things to right again, we all can rest a spell and enjoy some peace and quiet around here until the stages roll in tomorrow. You in a hurry, Julius, that you're not finishing your coffee?"

"No, no, Daisy," Julius Higgins protested, "just want to get started on that Eyetalian outfit. Miz Smith wants me to hitch up Bess, the slow jogger, 'bout eleven to take Millie sightseein', she said," and he left the kitchen.

"Well, I declare," Daisy said to an empty room, "that's right nice of Miz Smith. 'Pears she has the milk of human kindness in her bosom, after all. And Millie, poor mite, she

deserves a bit of time off. She's
been worked steady since she came.
But I'm going up and see Miz Smith
right now. Something don't add up.
Dishes can wait."

          She unhooked her apron and hung
it on the wall peg next to the stove.
As she went up the back stairs, she
could hear in the distance voices
coming from the taproom. She smiled.
"Sounds like George and Johnny are
here for the send-off."

CHAPTER 10

Two masked riders lurked in the grove of trees near the foot of Sand Hill. They had been there for some time, as the trampled ground beneath their horses' hooves testified, when one of the men warned "I think that's them acomin', Ame. Where's Julius? He was supposed to be here, too."

"I'll tend to him later," the other man promised grimly. "His fence-straddlin's gonna stop once and for all."

The carriage drew nearer, with the mare pulling it at a slow jog and one occupant gesturing as though conducting a tour.

"That's Phidia," Ame said. "She's downright good at play-actin'. Missed her calling, she did."

"Wish I knew half the time what you're talkin' about," complained his companion.

Ame, however, adjusting his mask, had spurred his horse to the side of the carriage and was shouting "Halt, or I'll shoot. Get down from there, Millie Cooper. You're going back where you came from. Get down, I say!"

Reaching into the carriage, he yanked at the sleeve of the other passenger. As he did so, the veil covering the face of the girl fell off. Ame gasped in surprise "You're not Millie! Phidia Smith, this is a doublecross. You'll pay dearly for this."

His curses were drowned by the other kidnapper's shouting

"Somebody's comin'--let's skedaddle!"
Suiting the action to the word, he
wheeled his horse and disappeared up
over the hill to the southwest.

Phidia had grabbed the whip out
of its socket and was belaboring Ame
about the head and shoulders. This,
combined with the fact that a body of
horsemen was indeed galloping to the
rescue, led Ame to beat a hasty
retreat himself up over the same hill
trail that his partner had taken.

Arriving on the scene a moment
later, Johnny and George, along with
Sol Bowen and the constable, found
Mrs. Smith comforting a shaken Molly,
with Bess, the mare, placidly
awaiting the restoration of peace and
security to her humans.

"Well, I must say, you took
your time," Phidia calmly asserted.
"How did you manage to hogtie
Julius?"

"Liv gave him a drink with
knockout drops in it," said Johnny.
"And Daisy spread the word," Sol
declared. "It's a good thing she
did. Some of us might have gone back
to bed."

George Elliott had been
investigating the scene. "I believe
there were only two of the
marauders," he said. "I wish I knew
the whole story so I could write it."

His wish came true that very
day, although he never published the
story, only sent it on to Audolph
Hearst in New York City with the
stipulation that it go no further
than Millie and Mrs. Hearst.

When the constable, having
nobody to take into custody, had
gone, the others went back to
Montgomery Hall, where the answer to

their questions sat in the kitchen with Daisy, calmly drinking the coffee she had poured for him.

"Now, Abijah, you just go ahead and tell the others what you've told me, and I think things will come out all right."

*** * * * * * * * ***

"Well," said Abijah, "it was this way---I don't rightly know how the Roots got involved with the Swamp Gang, but when my brother Ernie got snookered in, Lorenzo and Neva was tied up tighter'n a fly in a spiderweb. Their place was a cache for the loot in these parts. When Ernie couldn't stomach some o' their ways, the gang saw to it he met up with an accident. Phidia never was party to any of their shenanigans, but the gang wouldn't let her loose, so they strong-armed her into comin' down here to be a connection they could use to spot valuable animals stabled here. They got hold of Millie as another means of ridin' herd on Phidia, figurin' the girl bein' her niece, she'd make no false moves."

"What about Levi, Ab?" asked Johnny. "We know something must have happened to him at the Root place, because the trail ends there."

"I was gettin' to that, John. Daisy, could you jest warm up this coffee? My throat's parched."

Daisy obligingly moved from the circle of rapt listeners, stirred up the fire and pulled the coffee pot to the front of the stove.

Abijah waited for her to come back to the table and then continued his story.

"Levi came late one afternoon, et supper with us and then showed his

- 58 -

wares to the house. Lorenzo invited him to stay the night and Levi guessed he might as well. Us boys stabled the mare. She's good horseflesh, Sol, and I hope we can get her back for you.

"But there! I'm gettin' ahead o' my story!" Abijah was obviously relishing his place in the spotlight, but now he faltered and went on more slowly.

"This is the hard part to tell, folks, and I don't rightly know what the truth is. Howsomever, some time in the night, Levi took it into his head to come downstairs and go out to check on his goods. No tellin' why. Maybe he suspicioned things weren't right. Anyhow down he came and out to the barn in his nightshirt with candlestick in hand. When he got into the barn, he found the gang ransacking his goods. Ame told me this, I wasn't there. I was home in bed where an honest man ought to be. I never saw Levi again. Ame says he died of a heart attack. Mebbee so, mebbee not. I can't say. But he was gone, the carriage was gone and so was the mare. One thing's for sure. The gang figured Millie had heard Ame make that crack about nobody finding Levi and they gave Neva a hard time for sending Two-Bits out with the bucket of hot potatoes, even though they figured the girl couldn't put two and two together and come up with the right answer.

Now, one o' the reasons I went to work for the Roots was to keep an eye on Millie for Phidia and so I was real pleased when they decided to send the poor mite down here so Phidia could ride herd on her and keep her from talkin'."

"But Millie doesn't really know enough to put anybody behind bars," said Johnny.

"Millie knows Levi was there for the night and she saw his goods when he unpacked 'em in the parlour. She surely must know that the thimble I gave her came out of Levi's pack, although I paid good money on the spot that night. I did intend it for Phidia, but it seemed right to let Millie have a keepsake, so I gave it to her, feelin' sorry for her and all."

"Another thing--Neva asked to see the rug that Levi was bringin' up on special order. He showed it to her and didn't she set her heart on it! Levi could be pretty stubborn and put it back in his rig. I don't know, I'd hate to say, but maybe- no, I won't say it! Anyway, Millie knew the rug was there in the upper hallway, rolled up and bold as brass. Millie could make out a right smart case against those thieves, Johnny."

"So could you, Ab, so could you," Johnny said to himself. Aloud, he asked "Do you have any idea where they might have taken Levi's body, Ab?"

"Well, now, that's a conundrum, for sure. All Ame said was 'he'll never be found.' He said 'no body, no case.' Only he used some big words first."

"Habeas Corpus?" suggested Johnny.

"Near as I can remember," agreed Abijah.

"Where do we go from here?" the young apprentice lawyer asked of the group seated at the kitchen table.

"Maybe we could start by trying
to find my mare?" Sol Bowen wishfully
thought out loud. "Where's Julius,
Ike? Maybe he knows something that
would help us."

Abijah snorted. "He knows a
sight more'n you can guess, Sol. He
was sound asleep when I got here, but
he ain't around now. Prob'ly went
home. Now, Phidia, you better speak
up."

So urged, Mrs. Smith slowly
began to tell how the gang, through
Julius, had used her and Lizzie, his
sister, to report the arrival at the
Hall of valuable horses, which could
later be stolen after leaving the
livery stable.

"What bothered me most,
though," she explained, "was their
not giving Millie any schooling,
passing her off as not too bright."

"Millie's as bright as any of
us!" cried Molly. "They just kept
her down, that's all."

"Well, she'll get her education
now," said her aunt firmly. "Sarah
Hearst promised to see to that."

****

As Ame, the outlaw, had
remarked to Abijah, there was no
case, no corpse and no firm evidence
to prove a crime had been committed.

No information could be gained
from the Roots, as shortly after
these events, Lorenzo Root tripped
over a rolled-up rug in the upper
hall of his domicile, fell down the
stairs and broke his neck. Neva
disappeared.

Neither could Julius be
questioned. The Erie Canal yielded
up his body some days after the
attempted kidnaping.

Under the circumstance, Abijah
and Phidia and Lizzie were not held.
The first two announced their
intention to be wed and depart the
scene of their past.

John and Molly looked forward
to their own approaching nuptials and
in far-off New York City, Millie
embarked upon an entirely new life,
although she would always keep in
touch with Molly Maguire Dawley.

The Biermann's elected to stay,
but in Canajoharie. George Elliott's
poem was set to music, published and
subsequently, when The War Between
the States broke out, was used as a
popular marching tune by both sides
in the conflict.

In Fort Plain, the inhabitants
settled down to a rather hum-drum,
but largely appreciated normal life.

*****

Up on the hills, Calfurnia
Forte was regaling her mother with
some of the latest news:

"Lorenzo Root is dead, Ma. I
hear he tripped over a rug and fell
downstairs; broke his neck. Neva
hadn't finished housecleaning, so the
rug was rolled up yet and laying
right out there in the upstairs front
hall."

"H'm'ph!" her mother said. "I
never held with carpets, anyhow.
Take a sight o' cleaning come spring
ever' year."

Calfurnia bit her tongue. She
had been about to tell her mother of
the lovely Oriental rug that Henry
had ordered for her from Levi, the
traveling peddler. But then, Levi
hadn't shown up, so it didn't
signify.

"Well, then, this will make you

laugh, Ma: There was an Italian man around looking for relatives, they tell me. Imagine! Looking for relatives up here!"

"Why didn't he come and ask me?" Anne Shaul mildly remarked. "Your grandfather Tom always said he had a strain o' Eyetalian blood in him. And your name is Eyetalian. Califurny; name o' the wife o' Julius Caesar." Warming to the subject, she chuckled, "That ain't all I kin tell you about Eyetalian blood, either-----"

"Now, Ma," her daughter hastily cut her off, "we're having Injun Pudding for supper! You like that!"

****

Down at Montgomery Hall, Johnny was telling Molly how things stood in the case of Levi Hirsch, the missing peddler.

"Molly, I hate to admit it, but this outlaw Ame was right. no Habeas Corpus, no Corpus Delicti, no hard evidence, no case, period. It's back to everyday law for me. It was all for nothing, Molly."

"Not for nothing, Johnny. Millie's safe, George's poem is getting recognition and the Count is on his way back to Italy with an excellent impression of our peaceful valley."

"The jury's still out on that last, I think, my dear. But otherwise I agree with you completely." And Johnny sealed his verdict with a resounding kiss.

THE END